A LIFE OF POETRY

by Gordon Whitney

ISBN 978-1-7771117-3-1 (ebook)

ISBN 978-1-7771117-2-4 (paperback)

Cover by Kathy Whitney

For the students of Gladstone Secondary School, past and present, and budding poets everywhere!

CONTENTS

Why Poetry?

PREFACE

One day in 1962, when I was a senior mathematics teacher at Gladstone Secondary School in Vancouver, a sixteen-year-old student appeared in my Grade 10 math class. His name was Avo Erisalu, and he brought some of his poems to show me. I quickly realized he was a gifted poet. After I read and praised his work, he asked me, "Why don't you write poetry?" So in the following weeks, I did. When I handed over my poems to Avo for his perusal, he suggested we start a poetry magazine. We advertised for students to come forward with their poetry. Avo named our magazine *The Juggler*. It thrived for five years, producing five annual editions. I also encouraged the head of the English department, Ed Barton, to try his hand at writing poetry. Avo and I were fascinated by Ed's poems, and we included them in *The Juggler* too. Since those early days sponsoring the Gladstone poetry club, I have spent many happy hours reading other poets and writing my own poems. Now I am ninety-six years old, and I am still writing poems. Thank you, Avo, for inspiring all of us would-be poets!

A LIFE OF POETRY

LOVE

LOVE COMES SWIFT

Love comes swift
transcending heart
beat's prosaic tune
like robins singing
morning 'til evening
letting sweet music
fall on lovers' paths
promising love
unending.

Veins engorge red lips
swollen with wishes and
wild cries, and love sets
sensuous stones on paths
plucked and cherished
in lovers' hands.

Kiss trembling after kiss
time trembling after time
phallic blades held high in
lovers' heated hands yield
suddenly to seascapes of
bright blue eyes.

Such is love and may it ever be
for we have cause to be fearful
of life and its unending passions
now let us cast hesitancy aside
and revel in love's mystery.

LOVE SONG FOR CRICKETS

CRICKETS sing at night
chirruping shrill in cool air,
calling coquettish lovers, hidden under stones,
while stars that only twitter in the dusk
lean down and blaze like meteors,
jewelling the night sky.

Enthralled, they come,
black-enamelled cricket maidens,
impelled, slender-legged, high-heeled,
rushing to embrace brave soldiers,
who, combat-weary, near death,
grasp, enfold lusty cricket maidens,
ensuring the arrival of next year's
black-enamelled legions.

Next morning, cold, at dawn,
I find them, inert, on sand,
scattered warriors supine among stones,
grotesquely disarrayed amid corpses and pebbles,
pierced by Sol's lancing fingers,
desiccated by golden arrows of the sun.

and still, and still, and still

Crickets sing at night,
chirruping shrill in cool air,
calling coquettish lovers, hiding under stones,

and stars that only twitter in the dusk
will lean down and blaze like meteors,
jewelling the night sky.

STAR GAZER

WHEN I was two,
sleeping under summer skies,
I thought the stars were singing
sweet lullabies to me.
When I was two.

When I was three,
someone said to me,
it's not stars, only crickets.
when you're older, you'll see.
When I was three.

When I was four,
I knew that crickets sing
to lovers hiding under stones.
childish thoughts I put away.
When I was four.

Now that I'm old,
I gaze in wonder at the stars,
yearning to be two again.
I was wiser, then, by far.
Now that I'm old.

SPRING

Spring awakening,
Winter yields soft melting snow,
lovers stroll with caring eyes
among the apple trees,
along smooth paths,
on measured rows.

Tender fingers caress
smooth, green, apple branches,
holding hands, eagerly touching
buds, to bring to one more Spring,
beautiful pink-and-white apple blossoms
to sighing lovers' eyes.

This sweet
remembrance of the past,
is but a far-off, distant dream,
knowing a child-wished Spring
cannot, will not, ever
come again.

Summer's sunlit sadness
warns of Autumn's sure approach,
letting leaves fall, letting greenness fade,
approving Winter's coming,
sans serendipity,
once again.

LOVE AT FIRST SIGHT

LATE for the meeting, out alone in the hall,
should I offer a reason, or go in after all?
how to enter, what excuses to proffer?
diverted by a door opening, softly ajar.
a red-headed girl stepped into the light,
green-eyed and freckled, a beautiful sight,
exquisitely Gael, with her red Irish hair,
like a girl back in Erin, at a Sligo fair,
she came to me, pausing, much too near,
speaking softly, so no one but I could hear,
her task, she said, cake 'n' coffee prepare,
for the meeting—in discussion—back there.
my hearing left me, composure undone,
I wondered, should I not ask her name
for politeness, but my voice never came.
out of control, I reached out, I embraced her,
pressed her firm to my chest, and, yes,
kissed her full on her mouth. my instinct felt right,
then, I'm sorry, I'm sorry, I drew back, contrite.
it's all right, she murmured, and reached out
so gently, her fingers touching my hand
it's okay, she whisper'd, and our courtship began,
and lasted for sixty more years.

ODE TO SERENDIPITY

DAYBREAK!
sun rises
on the rim
of Lill'wat ridge
shining down
on Lillooet our
Cariboo
town

we glance up
from coffee cups
rims brightly haloed
iridescent in the
light of the
questing sun

as it crossed our valley
and shines on our faces
asking to see if we're
still in love

pleading, I ask her
are we still lovers?
yes, she says, we will be
till the end of time

ecstatically I tremble
and drown in the sea
of her Irish grey eyes

one day I may sit all alone
beneath a grey Autumn sky
or a cold Winter sun with
clouds drifting by over fields
once our garden of love?

what'll I do?
what'll I say?

Say life is a card game!
Serendipity's the dealer
day after day after day and
the hand we are dealt is
the hand we must play!

LOVERS' QUARREL

WHEN I text you
I feel next to you as
you read my words
When you text me
I feel next to you as
I read your words
But when we're together
you *taunt* me and say
it was *me* who first said
those three little words
        "I love you."
I reply, "*No, no, no.*
        It wasn't *me,*
        It was *you!*"
Isn't love a
many-splendoured
thing?
sometimes erotic
sometimes erratic

ADAM 'N' EVE

Eve, when
I text you,
I feel you
so next to me
as you read
my words

Eve, when
you text me
I feel myself
so next to you
as I read
your words

yet
when we are
together you
are distant

I can
only sense
your words
saying it was
me who

tempted
you in
in the
garden

I wish
God would
make up his
mind

LOVE IS AN OUTCAST

LOVE can be a loser
if death deals the hand
parting's the lost wager
youth cannot command
unconsidered when young
uncomforting in old age

No one can read the cards
someone can stack a deck
sometimes someone can
hide an ace up a sleeve and
keep death in check

Is there a guarantee
that love lasts forever
it may, but obeys
a gene's urge to beget
human life is temporary
"beget and forget!"

LOVE LOST

Love's a poor loser
when death deals a hand

Till Death Us Do Part
is payable on demand

Misunderstood by young
unbearable by the old

Oh, to be able to read cards
or to stack the deck

To play an ace up a sleeve
when death takes a seat

There is no safe bet, just
play the hand you've been dealt

HAPPINESS

IF happiness
comes knocking at my door
comes in for a look see,
hangs hat in hall
how've you been, okay?
good to see you,
chats awhile, then
must be on my way
again

Oh, oh!
he forgot his hat
not to worry, he'll return,
or we'll conjure him up,
invite him to come in,
another casual chat
a wagging of the chin
memories will be back
never give in

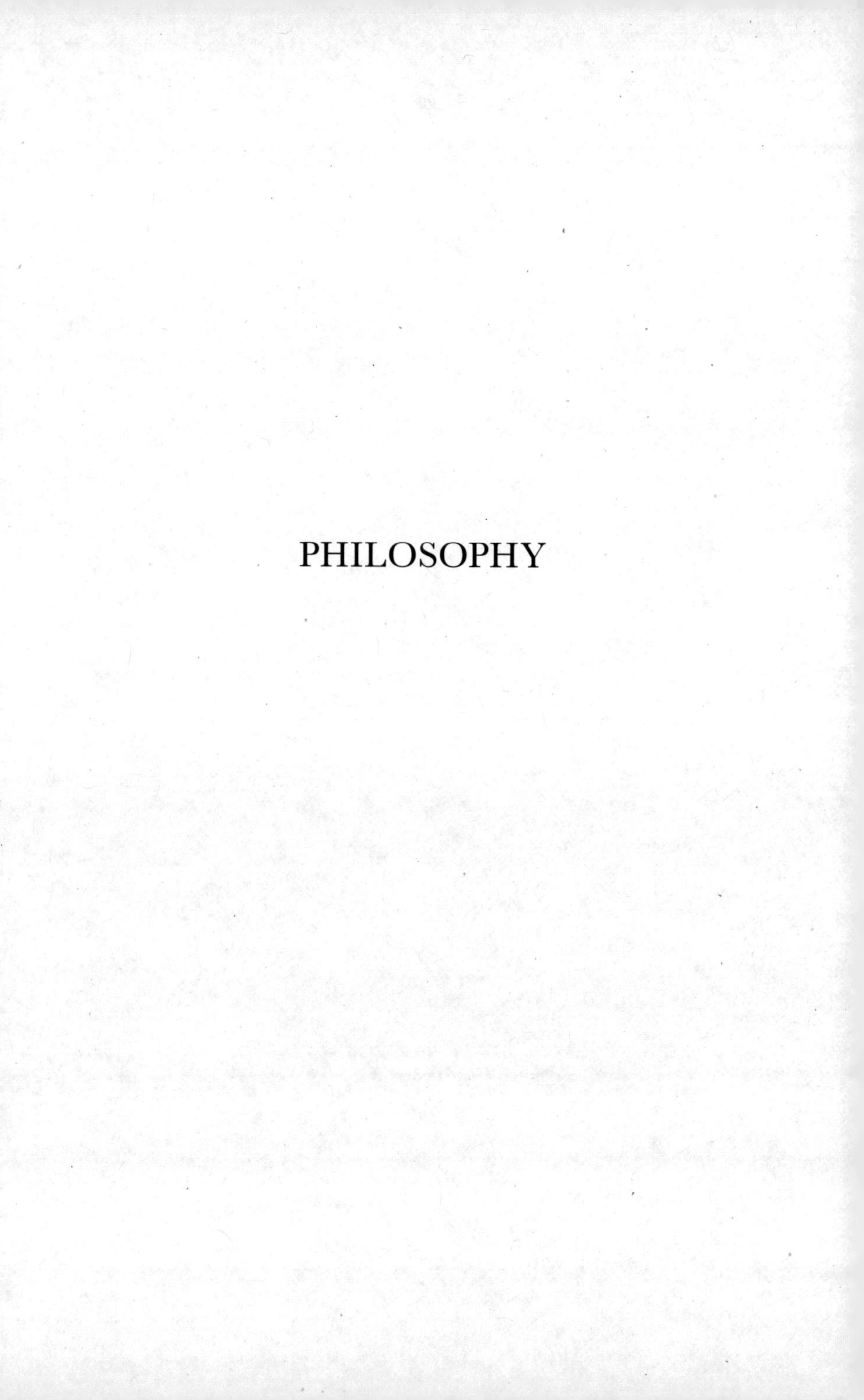

PHILOSOPHY

ATAVISTIC SONG

SUDDENLY someone knew
and I knew that I knew
that this is not the real it
that this is not the real me
that this is not the real anyone
          or you
          or anything
that this is some abstract
some dream in a young
afternoon and someone
is simply dreaming
          of this it
          of this you
          of this anything
and someone is asking if this means
any more than a dream did when
          anyone was young and small
          and that was a long time ago
          and anyone's bright toy
          and bouncing ball fell into
          and someone's arms held onto
          and real dolls talked and soft cloths
wove a bright someone's anyone cocoon
and someone is wondering whether anyone
could by simply awaking sometime leap back
          into someone's mother's womb
          with anyone's teddy and
          anyone's toys and
          anyone's pillow

onto someone's bright clean cloth
washed of anyone's enemy's hands
and cleansed of fear by someone
by the closing of the eyes of a dream

and if this is not anyone's real dream
and someone is not really dreaming
then this must be real and
    someone is real and
    someone is afraid and
    anyone is afraid knowing
    that terror sometime
    of no one trying to be
    someone and everyone
    knows that someone's dream
    is more real than any
    one man

WHERE HAVE OUR FORESTS GONE?

WHERE have all the forests gone?
burned in forest fires every one
when will big business ever learn
carbon-storing forests can't return?

Greenhouse gases in the air
global warming is everywhere
when will *we* ever, ever learn
fossil fuels *we* must not burn?

Big business's credo rules the day
first make a profit and then expand
more consumerism must be born
overpopulation plagues the land

One hundred years needed by CO_2 to go away
that's what our meteorologists say
why can't big business simply learn
there'll be no forests left to burn

Wake up big business, unplug your ears
more consumers means a lot more trash
polluting the planet while, on your rears,
you sit on fat assets counting your cash

LIFE'S A PASSENGER TRAIN

CONCEPTION
and birth and
a journey begun!
safe engineered
slow starting to run
hesitantly hesitant,
moderately speeding,
travelling, ravelling
kaleidoscope seeing,
soft seat relaxing,
rocketing rolling,
absolute fun!

Companion'ed in comfort,
family'ed in daylight
stranger'ed in half light
danger'ed in darkness
destiny known?
parentally shown?
solipsis-ly gazing?
sensuous we glide …
serendipity hiding …
yearning we ride …

suddenly … Stop!

Changing tracks?
Changing trains?

are we there?
no, we're here!
changing minds
once again!

Let's go back, let's return
to whence we became.
we can start, we can start
all over again!

No! we cannot go back
Albert Einstein rocks
and entropy rules!
only a train of thought
can a path regain!

SOL

Night after night, we unroll,
a winding sheet of infinitely
innumerable stars.

Day after day, we glare skyward,
staring blindly at a hot orange ball,
in an innocent azure-blue sky.

Were the Egyptians all wrong
to worship the sun?

We lie, camped, thin and naked, on a cold ground,
lulled to sleep, a cacophony of wheels whirring by,
pinned to earth by the unpitying stare of a star.

Dare we hope, by invocation or a bribe,
to secure a small promise it won't suddenly die?

RAIN

RAIN lies mainly on the plain
sing pretty ladies in Spain,
if it rains, "run for cover,"
I sing to myself and others,
"raindrops are falling on my head"
sings Butch Cassidy to the Kid

when the stars threw down their spears
to water heaven with their tears
did he smile his work to see?
did he who made a fluffy lamb
make soggy thee? asked Blake

rain is romantic to a
boy sitting puerile in a tent
on a rainy day bent on kissing
a sweetheart's lips so tears won't
dim her weeping eyes

every day wonderful rain blesses
trees, birds and bumbling bees
and if I suddenly ever feel dismayed
I just say, "rain, rain, rain, go away
and come again another day."

THE CIRCLE

GENESIS

Tree of knowledge
Living easy living lonely
Rib donated Eve created
Selfish gene apple eaten
Urging fig leaf purging
Woo and screw
Chaos born

EXODUS

Homo Sapiens
Adam proceeding
Mirror ego revealing
Question *life* demanding
Moses God is commanding
Moses stone laws carving
Life after death okay
Do not worry obey
Apocalyptic death
Planet and Man
Chaos reborn

(Sorry!!)

If you would make a circle
Go into it first and see how
You would do! (William Blake)

QUESTIONS

PENSIVE in an
afternoon sun
alder trees bending
shadows down on
boulders holding
creek bank boy
deep in thought
on granite
shoulder

creek cooling
barefoot toes
dangling touching
round pebble eyes
looking up at boy
eyes searching
for answers
what is life?
how did life
begin?

questions come
and questions go
pebbles in process
engage boy's eyes
pursuing ideas
in the universe of
his mind

did Galileo's lens
spite religion and suffer
to show us a scientific
path?

does Hubble's
telescopic eye reveal
an infinite universe's
trillions of galaxies
like our Milky Way?

can a Paramecium
swimming in a stale
raindrop teach us how
we learned to sense?

ANSWERS

DARWIN showed
life evolved by a
process of continual
adaptation to earth's
constantly changing
environment

marine biologists
observe unicellular
life forming in oceanic
hydrothermal vents.
observable processes
cannot be labelled
acts of creation

quantum theory
shows energy
becomes matter
becomes energy
becomes matter by
subatomic processes
ad infinitum

thermodynamics'
first law tells us
energy can
neither be created
nor destroyed

our Universe is all
energy in process

juggled words and ideas
tossed up to cloudy skies
echo back and puzzle his
questing mind however
wise men and wise women
declaim it is wisest to utter
we don't know

ROUAULT'S OLD KING

THE old king
Serene on the eve of death
Ordered robes and crown adorned
To pose for Rouault's bold brush
And looking on the artist as a friend
Spoke thusly

Paint me not as you see me now
But clench my teeth in anguish
For well I know the redness of my robe
Is dyed with blood from human hands

Unlink the ingots of my crown
That I refute the riches it accrued
And say instead I remember golden suns
Place a flower in one aching fist to say
Had I been free this would I cherish
And even give to you in payment for this task

Finally disjoint my limbs and reunite them
With your grotesque leaded brush to make
My subjects know that I was dead
When in truth to you these words I spoke
For no king in his right mind
Speaks thusly!

MAN WITH A HOE

I SEE my people
On new streets.
Their anger at my strangeness
Fills me with dread.

I am their old sequestered king,
Incognito among my people,
Who had hungered and were given cake
Instead of bread.

I proceed with immense regal calm,
Solemn, quiet, to a first dark corner,
And in heart-in-mouth fashion
Flee around it,

As if I had just read
Edwin Markham's
Poem,
"The Man with the Hoe."

GOD'S ERROR

THE things that you're liable to read
in the Bible ain't necessarily so
God created an unfirm firmament
Earth's core terrific volcanos spew
tectonic plates earthshake our planet
peaceful Pacific tsunamis create
Atlantic Ocean's icebergs threaten
Bermuda Triangles swallow ships
people and planes

Thermal vents vent cellular life
amoebas engulf jellyfish sting
selfish gene urges mass reproducers
asexual cells divide quick into zillions
people *sex*pand Earth overpopulates

Bacteria proliferate eat green plants
predation, predation, predation exists
fauna eat flora and flora eat fauna
plants proliferate jungles and climb
home for simians, man's early cousins
orangs and gibbons, gorillas, chimps
making tools to eat termites by probing
and bonobo bands perform a jungle
shaking resounding Nutcracker Suite

Axeless simians can't cut down trees
habitats intact evolution continues

eventual chimp brain enlarges and
Homo Sapiens is born and descends
stands erect, hands freed, scans horizon
sees future and invents super tools
stone hammer bow arrow and spear
masters *killing from a distance*
makes fire for Bronze Age and Iron Age
invents agriculture cum deforestation
food surplus civilizes overpopulation
pollution is massive habitat destroyed

Don't God's creations demonstrate
to all questioning minds
he's inept
gods make mistakes

WARRIORS

WALKING my garden path
checking cabbage plants
confronted daily by
white-winged warriors,
challenging my right to spy
on them as they search for
safe egg-laying sites on
hapless leaves, bases for
green caterpillar armies
to issue forth and munch
green chlorophyll across
innocent cabbage leaves,
where, once sated, they
will attach and hang inert
beneath leafy undersides
morphing into chrysalids
waiting, waiting, awakening
as wonderful white-winged
butterflies!

what a wonderful war
for the price of a few
leaves of cabbage

TIME PASSING

JOANNE

SPRING, the softening of Winter,
letting us stroll with caring eyes,
among apple trees walking
familiar paths fingers caressing
smooth green branches,
hand-holding, searching,
green buds to wish upon,
bringing forth again
white-pink sweet
blossoms we
loved

A sad sweet
remembrance of the past
is only a distant dream,
and now Spring, child wished,
cannot, will not, come again
Summer's sunny sadness will prevail,
warning of approaching Autumn,
letting leaves fall, letting greenness fade,
all-approving of Winter's arrival,
sans serendipity
once again

TIME PASSING

Look, they have faded
Camelias and chameleons now brass
Remember how they fleshed on stalks
With leaves like lizards climbing stems
And flowers flamed, bending the wind

With fragile red roses still defiant
To morning's yellow sun
In a China garden

Look, he has withered
Ripe grass coarsened, shaking in the wind
Remember how he fletched his limbs
He was alive, his arrows had desire
His lips aflame set other lips on fire
Now he sits memory's cup in hand
Fragile in a lonely China
Garden

see how they bend
our grassy ways
as we pass

FRASER RIVER AGATES

Spring and Summer die
and boys run naked
through Indian Summer
stepping stone to stone

cutting clay banks down
to frantic edges of
Autumn's Fraser
town

gray water washing
bronzed bodies raft
to islands lit by cold
September's sun

agates plucking at
bent over children's eyes
smoothed by time and
children's hands

glowing beckoning
from sifting sand
snug in memory of
thirty-seven agates

thirty-seven years
and one more each
September sun
come round

42

I must return them
to Indian Summer
let them feel again
child's eager grasp

for I am old and
grown weary of
memory's pleasant
game

TROUT LAKE

MEMORY peering sad
at Trout Lake Park
crow nesting heaven
crossing Burrard Inlet
foresting North Shore
climbing Grouse Grind
gaping at twin Lions
piercing bright sky
posing regal staring
down on Trout Lake
encircling path of grey
clay hardened by Nikes
passing northeast corner
passing tall green reeds
summer nesting home
for raucous Redwing
Blackbirds

that was long ago
when trout swam
in Trout Lake
before toilets flushed
and algae bloomed
and children dove
into *blue* water
and came up *green*

CHILDHOOD LOST

I HAVE descended an inner stair
with easy steps to a prison where
a child's voice slings pretty stones
to ring and echo against the sky

Come incarcerate me in a spell
benumb my ears to forget there
is a knell in each bell that rings
and casts itself to crack and die

To where all I will know is the press
and tug of a small child's hand
caressed dynamic of my flesh and
well-loved rhythmic of my bones
and let my fear drown in swells
of happy sounding bells
which children still will ring
enmeshed in joyous tones

You will say I am a fool to hide
behind small fragile sounds
from that fierce sooth I know
one quick hour will soon come round

Will those childish bells ring again
one small moment, then go untold?
bring me the opiate that I may forget
that the old child too, too soon grows old!

OLD AGE

THEY say Old Age
dulls our senses and
they say eyes fail
to see in detail
what they ought
I wonder if my brain is aging
and sometimes fails
to think a lovely thought

I wonder why my hearing fails
and an apparatus needs
a scientific modern touch
that helps me sort the sounds
but cannot help me much
when I need that special word
heard when I was young
a name, a man, a woman
who said or did some
wonderful thing

oh well
so it goes
yesterday I almost
smelled a marigold
tomorrow, maybe I'll
almost smell a rose

MEMORIES

I HAVE descended
by an inwound stair
with uneasy steps
to a prison where
memory fills my cell
with the sounds of
children's voices

Voices, happy echoes
playroom walls faded
dimmed by the warp
of time and sorrow's
persistent frown

Sunlight's memory,
greyed under clouds
of sadness, covers a
once-upon-a-time
blue sky

I ask myself
each time
where is the
key?

THE RAINBOW

FROM a chockum tree
a slender wand
tied to a line
hook fastened
cricket bait for trout
floated on the stream

A rainbow trout swims
to me in my dream
is caught and
it struggles in my hand
I saw its eyes cloud over
as I lay it on the sand,
with unseeing eyes, I see
a rainbow fade and die

I wake from my dream
tears bedim my eyes

Mankind's inherent urge
to hunt and kill, I know
I forgive our savage acts
inured to sleep I go
no one weeps, no keening sounds
a rainbow fades and dies

Old age, forgive me
Wishing, alone, can't
Make man wise.

SECOND COMING

OLD Dan
had an idea
that the Messiah
would come back
dressed like
a bum

He'll
come to us
looking like me and you
and say just one word
and the world
will stand
on end

Old Dan
tested this idea
many many times
and one day it
happened just
as he said

He's here, *He*'s here,
He's gonna speak to me,
He's gonna say the *Word*,
Listen!

"Please, Dan,
can you spare a
dime?"

Do rich people think
He'll drive by
in a limo?

A TRAGEDY?

A POCKET knife
A willow branch
A slender wand
Fishing rod held
By human hand

A hook and line
Cricket bait cast
Bright green pool
Shiny trout caught
And held in hand

Stricken rainbow
Fading fast in sun
Shivers and dies
Lies still on stone
Its life undone!

now old and wise
should I condemn
such human acts
so earthly rash
so un-sublime?

no, we're not
from heaven sent
by miracles of birth
bearing Adam's curse
we are evolved!

woman and man
we disdain to claim
an origin from above
we're earthbound cousins
to the orangutan!

THE DREAM

WHERE in dreams can a pretty path lead?
Will danger be waiting 'round a bend?
Will sadness or gladness greet me there?
Will the future bring a sad or a happy end?

A voice says, "Go to bed 'n' see!"
I acquiesce and supine I pray,
"Now I lay me down to sleep with
Serendipity at my feet,
Help me find Innisfree today."

To a cabin I'm led and I find
A broken door hinges unhung
"Don't Enter!" glares from a wall
Inside a phonograph is playing
Errors I don't want to recall
Can't we ever avoid bad dreams?
Can't Father Time mend them?
Dare we confront and end them?
Yes, just yell, *"Good memories, live!*
Bad memories, die!" then click on
Scan and *Select* and press
Delete and wave *Goodbye.*

CHRISTMAS

CHRISTMAS TREE

JINGLE bells jingling, ringing clear,
Excited, just seven more days,
Christmas, once more, will be here.
Where oh where, is our tree?
From its cardboard tomb, it calls,
Over here, over here, come see!
Look, it's there, sad, unjointed tree
And where to put it, where will it stand?
Over there? No, right here! all agree.
Our tree now rejointed lifted installed
Its pedestal intact and against the wall

Branches joined, standing so tall.
Beautiful green, enchanting us all.
We are your servants, dear tree,
We'll weave your branches, you'll see,
With our elder hands as onward we go
To your stems and fronds, soon with care,
Our hands will fresh fir needles sew.
Then around you, dear tree, we'll all dance,
Spinning, and turning and prancing with joy,
Each woman, each man, becoming once more,
A new Christmas girl, a new Christmas boy.

O TANNENBAUM

O TANNENBAUM, O Christmas Tree,
So alive and green your branches be,
Fresh raised up from your yearlong sleep,
By gentle Gemini hands that keep,
Your sparkling lights so loving wrapt
With coiled wires and points intact.
To ensure again our star will shine,
With treetop joy at Christmas time.
Among your branches, we will go
On stems fresh green fir needles sew,
Restring branches with coloured lights,
Shiny ornaments and candy delights
Our hearts aglow with Christmas pride,
Around you then, we'll dance with joy,
Each woman and man again become
A Christmas girl, a Christmas boy.

FIRST CHRISTMAS PRICE CRESCENT

I SEE you all around the tree,
As if it were yesterday…
My family, whole at last, my dream,
Siblings and cousins roughhousing, enjoying
All the pleasures of this season,
Photos, there were many,
Against a glittering background of new-fallen snow
We sat down that night, all eleven of us,
For the very first time
And raised our glasses
The tinkle of crystal
Ringing in our newfound joy.
Secretly, I prayed and hoped
It would ever be so.

CHRISTMAS ANGEL

LATE from the party? Christmas tree scan!
Everything in order? Bulbs burning bright?
You check the left, I'll check the right!
Halfway in scanning, serendipity attends
A delightful vision, shiny bauble ascends
A beautiful woman with dazzling blue eyes
Pops out from green branches, Christmas surprise!
My faltering logic, my hasty assessment
My rapid conclusion?
That beautiful face just has to be an
    Angel in disguise
Or maybe I just had too much wine
At the office party?

A CHRISTMAS WITCH

STRINGING
silver strands
on boughs
peering at him
hanging up
glass globes
unaware that
she wonders
can I make him
peer forever
into my bright
blue witch's
eyes

recalling
eyes are
portals to
the soul
she knows
face to face
she can cast
a spell and
drown his
soul deep
in the sea
of her
eyes

through
branches
face to face
she sends a curse
he falls enslaved
she commands
him rise
he gasps
you are, you are
a beautiful woman

she smiles removes
her blue jean disguise
refastens her batwings
invisible to human
eyes

BUTTERFLY

ONE never quite knows what a leaf can hide,
(As Adam discovered in the Garden of Eden)
But once, as a boy, a miracle I found,
In my very own flower-cum-vegetable ground,
As I cautiously upturned a black currant leaf,
To find what was warping its soft underside.

Ah! I spied a green caterpillar clinging there,
Munching, inverted, on its chlorophyll home.
Stupidly, I touched it, it froze, then continued,
Digesting its way to its chrysalis zone, where,
Morphing, its atoms would make it become
An exquisitely beautiful butterfly clone.

But enough! We all know what butterflies do,
Gemini's secret should intrigue us all too.
Nadia, manager of our Gemini tower, is a
Chrysalis-cum butterfly, worker bee too.
Our perfect superintendent, plain-dressing Nadia
As chrysalis obvious, as butterfly unseen.

But luck, only yesterday, came suddenly our way.
Over coffee, we suddenly looked up to see,
Beautifully dressed Nadia fly through the door,
Bright-blue eyes, dark suntan, I swear she had wings,
As she floated among us, I shouted to the sky,
At last, at long last, we have our own butterfly!

LILLOOET TOWN

LILLOOET ODYSSEY

AND I came to this place
borne against my will
as if I had been flung over mountains
by Chagall

In a darkly blowing wind

I have been here before I said
the pale backwash of windswept trees
the boulder-strewn flats
        all seem familiar
        and strange
        and the trees
        shedding their bark
        letting fall amber tears
        and snakelike scales
        in discarded heaps
        pointing their fingers
        at the town
        derogatory

                even the dogs
                cringe and
                slink by

This old Cariboo goldrush town
only look at it then or look at it now

            unpainted houses
            roofs perfunctory and patched
            in front where it shows
            clotheslines sagging across
            grey front yards
            chickens in porches
            fence pickets scattered
            firewood drifting in piles
            while children play
            at poor games
            in a small dust

to feel the deep unsatisfying contour of it all
to see nature stumbling on Saturday streets
            shoulders burrowing their way uptown
            and down and the-the-the-
            only human warmth coming from
            chimneys, guy-wired in air, their
            blue smoke charring pale lips
            as they walk and talk a monosyllabic
            eh-eh-eh-eh

And I came to this place
borne against my will
as if I had been flung over mountains
by Chagall

THE OLD CHIEF

O CHIEF,
Your bones lie bare in shawls of sand
Bereft of feathers fine sprung
From copper discs now green in age
Your arms unbanded legs unsheathed
From shells, quills, sun-shattered beads
Buckskin and a hundred scattered ornaments
Your ribs' lyre in a willow wind
Your once beat heart chokecherry seed
In sand your bones unmarrowed now
Spew out love wind-tossed away
For that once-beauty maid
Who honed the blade of your
Desire

Your two ghosts peer
From those blind socket eyes
Her lips moan with yours as willows weep over
Your two voices rustle summer maize as
Two stalks rusk together in a hot wind and
Gaunt carpal bones that clutch an argillite pipe
Once held a flesh-hard hand against a lover's
Thigh

O Chief,
Your smile glints from sagebrushed sand
Your skull grinning thunder in a clay sun
For secrets lie within your ochred bones

Your flesh has stirred that earth awhile
And now when horse-worn trails mound your grave
You thrust through wounds wisely
Flowers out of
Dust

DEATH OF A SMALL CHILD

THE Indian village greets the rising sun
voices wailing through aspen trees under a blue sky.
below, Lillooet townspeople waken and listen sadly.
compassion echoes off grey roofs up into white trees.

Indian men women children stand and wail
keening loudly under a Cariboo mourning sky
eyes sad and hollowed out by tears for one child
taken away too sudden into death's easy hands

"Do they wail to appease the spirits' returning?"

"No, the Land of Death holds tribal mysteries,
telling us how to grieve over the death of a small child
so innocent and so young."

Mount Brew bends its late afternoon shadows
embracing fear to ease the longing for love
and the drying of tears and accepting of pain
caressing the buckskin moccasin–trodden ground

Weary dogs lie comatose in cool shade
Lil'wat women tend their cooking fires
tear-streaked faces cooled by a Cayoosh breeze
blowing softly over sweet-smelling sage.

"Why, Shaman, do Lil'wat people wail to an
empty sky?"

"Why, O White Priest, do Lillooet people wail in a
wooden church?
We Lil'wat people talk to God straight up in a real sky.
He hears us!
Can God hear you pray to Him under your church's
heavy wooden sky?"

"Why, O White Priest, do Lillooet people wail in a
wooden church?

LIL'WAT LAKE

ONE hundred twenty
degrees in the
          sun!
one hundred ten
degrees in the
          shade!

but no shade!
on Lillooet's dusty blazing
wooden-sidewalked
          streets

two boys
squat inert in
maple tree shading
safe from blazing
Cariboo July's hot
summer sun

two broken promises
          too hot to pick
     ripe apricots
two mothers
          waiting to can
     in widemouth Mason
          jars

as smug half-ripe
peaches peacefully
gaze and smile at pink
Joe Pizzi roses blooming
in flowerbeds cooled and
damp from sprinklering
this blazing July's
Main Street
day

Ohhhhhh, to float again
all afternoon in sky-blue
Lil'wat's Seton Lake deep
cool water drowning
in summer
dreams

PLACER MINERS

SILHOUETTED against the sky
placer miners huddling around
a sluice box standing innocent
among boulders mud sand gravel
on a Fraser River bar below Lillooet
Cariboo's mile zero
     town
yellow cottonwood leaves fall
upon rock-strewn damp sand beneath
a bleak September afternoon sun
on ground worked and reworked by
legions of long gone and long forgotten
Chinese miners in the gold rush of
     1849
like tintype photos hanging
on a museum wall picturing miners
momentarily poised at rest in their
search for elusive layers of sand and
gravel-bearing gold, a hopeful fortune
of fine gold particles deposited thousands
of years ago by a Pleistocene
     glacier
placer miners mimicking a glacier
washing water and gravel over a screen
letting sterile stones roll by to the ground
as heavy gold particles pass through brotherly
black sand waiting to be laundered sorted
and surrendered at long last into
weary placer miners'
     hands

BLUE BOULDER

SITTING there
guarding
trout-filled
blue-green pool

watching
Cayuse Creek
roaring down
from Duffy Lake
grinding
bump bumping
click click clicking
polishing rounding
Cretaceous
stones

plunging frantic
into the abyss
Cayuse canyon
narrowed wetted walls
frenzied passageway
    tortured turnings
    ricocheting lunging
    three-mile
    passionate
    ride

finally ...
        exhausted!
        weary
        slow-moving
        Cayuse Creek

ignominious
surrenders
to ancient
muddy
malevolent
maternal
Fraser River

STONE FLY

Ice water
    runs on stones
        and stone fly falls
            crawling legs of water

Tails fork
    in splices
        and fish bend shafts
            of cold suns

Knees clutching
    toes in cold dampness
        rubber-legged we stand
            hands caught in traps

A fish impatient tugs
    at sleeves of stone
        jumping feet over
            away from hooks

        to a quiet
        deep
        green
        pool

NIGHT BIRD

AWAKE
cool night
Moon rising
setting slow
in top of
tree

Moon
sinking
in branches
escaping
my mind
my sleepy
eye

sudden
night bird
holding
Moon
high in beak
beckons me
come
near

I reach up
fingers curl
grasping
empty
air

night
bird
calmly
opening
beak

drops
yellow
Moon

into
my
hand

GRANDMOTHER

GRANDMOTHER crashed
past lintels, clutching and
apoplectic
    fell
        down

a last breath rattled
over boards as eyes
gently opalesced
and went out, our house
left agonizing
     under
        sudden
           death

on a stilted unhinged parlour door
she posed in Sunday dress
with arms rigor-mortised across
lifeless breasts and vases of
blue Hydrangeas pouring air
full of sweet-scented death
     on closed
        ears and
           eyes

neighbours sit in chairs
round-fearing eyes kissing corpse
and speaking funeral parlance

of her and those others
their own voice proof they were
on this side still
"all must go sometime," they said,
their secret glad
    it was
        still alive

now, when I pass by graves,
headstones leer and lean together
and plot furtively in pale-green grass
while blue hydrangeas turn blue eyes
    on me, a knowing
        sick sweet
            smile

DEATH OF A PEACH TREE

APRIL
peach tree blooming
alongside new fence
blossoms floating
in air

June
peaches ripening
smiling in the sun
rejoicing even
in rain

July
peaches softening
heavily on branches
quietly begging to
be picked

August
neighbour shouting
branches on her side
of new fence must
be removed

New neighbour
offering hand in peace
new friends can share
peaches both sides
of fence

Irate neighbour
runs in wrath to tree
shakes down peaches
showering hate on
barren ground

One late dark night
peach tree secretly
silently anonymously
foolishly cut
down

BOY

Boy crouches hidden smug under sky
silent, alert, roaring creek rushing by
hugging damp gravel, rod by his side
secretly peering through branches that hide
him from five rainbow trout on patrol.

the biggest one, pool master, unaware
of Boy's presence and cool killer stare
relaxes and focusses on food passing by
hungering for larval caddis flies stirred
up from stones by Duffy Lake's stream
descending to the Fraser below.

Boy secretly assembles his gear
threading a grasshopper body
from his pocket bait box onto
a snelled fishhook, size number ten
one head, one thorax, one tail, two legs
five grasshopper body parts for five
hungry trout. Amen!

Boy hooks and lands all five trout in a row
placing them neat in his gunny sack creel
picking up his rod, he heads back to the road
emerging just in time as tourists drive up,
"Any luck?" they implore. Boy shakes his head.
"This creek is all fished out."

MY CAT

ONE morning
we went fishing
my cat Woody 'n' I

he rode upon
my shoulder, he
watched me tie a fly

I caught a fish
he jumped right down
ate it 'n' meowed, "Goodbye!"

I should've taught 'im
some table manners
maybe I'll do it, by 'n' by

LILLOOET: HOMEWARD TO THE CARIBOO

BENCHES of grey sand backed by clay bluffs
    for memory to sit sad upon
      and see itself

trudging in tennis shoes toe-holed and worn
clumping along flats barren and burned as
sagebrush and loneliness sit side by side
searching for shade beneath ponderosa pines
for a life-giving shelter beneath a hot sun
        in July

sitting in pale backwashes of glacial boulders
sitting beneath tall pines that blister and weep
stung by the rays of a black mud-wasp sun with
pine needles twisting and agonizing in flesh and
conjuring up flashes of an extraordinary ordinary
      blue sky

a boy possessing a power to love such a land
savouring sweetness where others find salt
a stranger knowing all strange things that pass
those mysteries and dreams that gleam on a
      jackknife blade

a pair of deft wondrous hands pressing edges
of a lifetime together, sharp-fingered but unbled
in the aliveness in the nearness and in the now
as one grows old and multiplies while others
      drain their eyes

blackcap chokecherry and soapallalies bloom again
colorful sweetness begging to be picked as they
huddle under hillsides that crumble like the chalk
       of old bones

while below, the river serpentines and unwinds
and twines a grey that splits the house in two
half-dead with the corpses of cows and boys and
cowboy Indians in July riding their pink silk yellow
red and green bandanas up and down the streets of
      of the vanished horseback
          town

LILLOOET REUNION

UNNOTICED by the hills
by Red Rock Fountain Ridge
Mount Brew and Fraser River
and battered Cayuse Creek
by frigid BC Hydroed
Seton Lake
our two legions are assembled
in old Doc Stewart's
legion hall

from here and there
and everywhere, we meet
dear friends, all loved and
lovely in old age
gathered here
together

our names
begin and fall
and summon up old pages
dim-sketched on our past
while memory draws cards
and wins a poker hand
and then

we each recall
our words come back
to bounce to bubble up and say

you do remember don'tcha
we do, we say, we do
remember
when
and
then
at our command
the good old days
arise and resurrect

old arrows, pipes and argillites
and pitted stones and needle bones
dissecting old cadavers
by wanderings and
pursuits of

daily lives
of daily breads
and trespasses and yes
forgive us our trespasses
we scour and excoriate
our Fraser River–bedded
time
no, no, no, not that
Eastern Mountain Time
that Standard or Pacific time
but fast-flowing slow-burning
Fraser River Time
the time-of-your-life
time

and then
compassioned we recall
those gone-on-ahead-friends
we-hope-to-see-you
old passionate loves and lovers
those can-we-ever-hope-again
to-meet-you
even
in our
dreams

and then
on cue
Old Father Time
friend-unfriendly father
old trusted-untrustworthy pal
stops
relents and gives us
time for plenishings and
reminiscings

and Old Man Lillooet
father of us all, yes all, yes all
awakes
blinks
stretches
yawns
and rises
and pauses
and chuckles

and grins

at at at at at

the naming of his children

the praising of his kin

the laughing at his jokes
the peering at his pictures
the touching hands therein

and Main Street stridings
and back alley strollings
and gravestone gazings

sad sad sad
and so amazing

we are
once more
those long-ago once-again children
lifting our faces to the sun
like fresh pink Joe Pizzi
summer garden
roses

we stand agaze
and pluck the petals
as they fall

and softly settle
safe on memory's lap
and
brush away tears
brush aside years
temporary permanently
passed-by years

and then
and then
we call the roll
and recognizing us, us, us and us
we question-answer-question, go
spinning round and round the room
tiptoeing through the tulips and
table-hopping hop-scotch treading
stones of sweet
memory

and
oh and oh and oh
remembering too
don't cry don't cry don't cry
how young how young how young
how very very young
we were

and then
time slows and stands aside
and quickens our stride and

lets us skip and run and
dance frenetic to our laughter
as joyfully we read
our lists

and name our
names and games
reciting stories and events forgotten
how we bobsledded winter's snowy hills
and skate again on Fraser's ponds
and cardboard slide the icy dips
the big and little dips
until

at last
we come to know
time doesn't mind or even care
that we've grown old
and thinned our ranks
and greyed our hair
or lined our faces
with despair
it only minds
we are!

and
lastly last of all
that early-yawning morning after
meeting one last time
in Lou's drive-in on Main

that-ham-and-eggs-and-toast-and
breakfast coffee-cup café
we drink our last goodbyes
and say

it is, it is, it is
the time to leave
and must we must we must
return to heres and nows
and travel to our faraways and
so reluctantly
we stand
and pause
and

clasp our
fondest hands
and say this
was the best
the very, very best
and promise

we can, we will, we shall
return to Lillooet
come what may
another
day

WHY POETRY?

POETS

POETS, musicians
with words and airs
transcend life's tedium
with poetry and song.

We, labouring persons,
academic, mundane,
condescending for all,
sustenance maintain.

So our poets, musicians
can beauty ensnare,
artistic inventions and
potions prepare.

To beguile us, to twirl us
with dancing and song,
romancing and loving
our whole lives long.

Poets, musicians, rare spirits
disguised, flesh and bone
returned from our pasts,
new worlds to clone.

POEMS, MUSIC

MUSICIANS and poets
with poems and airs
transcend our worlds
banish our cares.

We in our labours
academic, mundane
their labours ensure
sustain and maintain.

So cherished musicians
can symphonic fare
and bel canto arias
and ballets prepare.

Poets evoking images
can coax sadness away
awake, happy thoughts!
carpe diem's here to stay!

Poets and musicians
bear our hearts along
with joy never ending
in poetry and song.

POETRY

POEMS
short, didactic
narrative and long,
rhythm and rhyme
may still carry on.

Poems
plucking heartstrings
rouse lovers' sighs,
iambic pentameter
still may comprise.

Poems
dolorous, weeping
teared faces assign
rhyme and rhythm
dismayed, resign.

And that is one story
of rhythm and
rhyme.

STILL LIFE

MELONS by Picasso,
mandolin concerto,
melon sliced in two becomes
two harlequins who strum
and pluck at pizzicato seeds,
no frets, no fretting needs,
but bowls of beauty rich and mellow,
flesh tones overflowing yellow,
magic music's hum resounding,
jewelled fly comes buzz-arounding
to suck dry hollowed sugary skins,
monuments to empty mandolins,
and when a fly ascends,
a concert ends.

DILEMMA

MORNING half-light dawning,
Leaves, bedewed, glistening,

Sunlight struggling through branches,
Lovers twined, tentedly sleeping,

Rudely awakened by the sun now risen,
Freed, once again, from the bondage of night,

One lover sighs for tomorrow's rose,
One lover weeps for the rose of yesterday.

Whose dream should we follow?
Which one shows the way?

CARPE DIEM

Morning sun's caresses,
Sleeping lovers awake.

One yearns for tomorrow,
One weeps for yesterday.

Whom should we follow?
Which shows us the way?

Neither sighs nor tears,
Can happiness ensure.

Carpe diem! Carpe diem!
Let us live for today!

POETASTER

HIGH priest, why
do you not
write poetry?
you appoint yourself
to pulpits up and down
the island and you
minister to these
dusky maids of
song!
you receive
confessions, you
forgive and extol
their virtues which
you own!
you must
unfrock yourself
in their presence
rub salt hands
blessing on their
lithe bodies
leave off adoration
from afar and take
a maid or two
to bed!

PROSE

PROSE,
a journey,
sometimes brief,
sometimes long,
author as guide,
words carry along,
landscapes, skyscapes,
seascapes, flowing like a tide,
disembarked, journey's end,
leaves readers sated,
satisfied.

POETRY II

PROSE,
a gourmet dinner,
plated images passing by,
mind ingesting flavours,
saved in memory as they fly,
pretty sweet dishes come smiling our way,
exhilarating, enjoying, disappearing,
digesting memories, pleased to stay,
gathered and saved, whenever to send,
a satisfying prose repast,
a satisfying end.

ACKNOWLEDGMENTS

I would like to thank Diane Van Dyke, Paul and Val Bjarnason, Nadia Romanovskaya, Pat Gillan, and Angie Price for reading my poems and commenting on them. My daughters, Kathy and Laurel, helped me with the art, layout, and editing of this book.

ABOUT THE AUTHOR

Gordon E. Whitney was born in 1925 in Lillooet, BC. He graduated from UBC in 1947 and began his thirty-four-year teaching career at Gladstone Secondary School in 1951. During those years, he sponsored the Gladstone Poetry Club, which published *The Juggler*, Gladstone's annual poetry magazine. Gordon presently lives in Qualicum Beach and will celebrate his ninety-seventh birthday in December 2022.

He welcomes comments from his readers. Find him at gewhitney.com.

ALSO BY GORDON WHITNEY

In 2020, Gordon published *Boyhood Memories of a Cariboo Town: Lillooet Stories*, a collection of short stories about his youth in the 1930s.

Information about his book and his interviews is available at gewhitney.com.